1 MONTH OF
FREE
READING

at
www.ForgottenBooks.com

ISBN 978-0-260-99413-4
PIBN 10999250

TO THE CLASS OF 1953:

Soon you are to join the long list of graduates who for more than a half century have gone from our college to become professional teachers. Never has our country needed teachers, educated and trained, as it does today. It will be your responsibility to pass on the great cultural and ethical heritage of our Western Civilization. It will be your duty to implant a working faith in the freedom of Democracy and to develop another generation who can think freely, clearly and without prejudice, and with sustained wills bring to reality in personal and social living the Faith of our Fathers.

The College has striven to give you knowledge and vision, and the beginning practice in the Art of Teaching. Out of the experience of the college years, you may grow to full stature as a person and make your own contribution in the creation of a world free and more secure.

May you meet the challenge of living courageously and never give up when problems seem insoluble.

I wish you success in every undertaking.

GROVER C. BOWMAN
President

"Within his gay and sparkling eyes
a wealth of understanding lies."

DR. EUGENE FREEL

To you, friend, counselor, and guardian angel, we dedicate this record of our four years in college. We cannot
hope, in these few words beneath your picture to begin to
express the wealth of warmth and affection we feel for you.
Only when we, as teachers, begin to guide the faltering steps
of youth can we hope to repay the debt we owe to your kind
heart and eternal patience. Knowing you has truly been a
privilege.

THAT WHICH WE KNEW, AND LOVED--OUR COLLEGE

Taconic Hall

College Hall

FACULTY

TRAINING SCHOOL FACULTY

"The guardians of that last league before our dark
ship landed on a favored shore"

FIRST ROW: Helen E. Brown, Grade Four; Helen E. Mallery,
Grade One; Viola Cooper, Grade Five; Claire M. Barry,
Junior High; Margret Stevenson, Grade Two. SECOND ROW:
Harold H. McLean, Junior High; Loretta J. Loftus, Grade
Three; John A. Durnin, Principal; Mary Walsh, Grade Six;
John S. Sullivan, Junior High.

COLLEGE FACULTY

"their gentle hands were at the helm as we
did homeward journey o'er the wine dark sea."

FIRST ROW: Ames S. Pierce, Social Studies; Dr. Dayton N. Dennett, E.._glish; Harry L. Crowley, Mathematics; Edmund K. Luddy, Social Studies. SECOND ROW: Mary Underhill, English; Beth E. Weston, Dean of Women; Bertha Allyn, Senior Clerk; Margret M. Lanoe, Librarian; Dr. Hazel B. Mileham, Director of Training. THIRD ROW: Wallace H. Vennable, Science; Dr. John Semon, Science and Mathematics; Dr. Grover C. Bowman, President; Lillian E. Boyden, Music; Dr. Eugene L. Freel, Psychology; Harry Willis, Bookkeeper. ABSENT: Martha E. Durnin, Education; Andrew S. Flagg, Dean of Men.

SENIORS

GRAHAM KENNETH ANDREW

"Who in understanding is beyond all

Intramural sports 1, 2, 3, 4; Drama Cl
"Three-Cornered Moon"; Glee Club 3,
mas Carol", "Mikado"; Taconic Col
College Fellowship 4; College Publicit
book Staff 3; Editor 4; Press Club 3;
Publicity 3, 4.

CAROLYN GRACE BENNETT

"You are the pearl among wom

W. A. A. 1, 2, 3, 4; Class Treasurer 3; D
4; Glee Club 1; "Christmas Pageant'
Events Club 2; College Fellowship 4; Hc
cil 2, 3.

JANET ELIZABETH BISHOP

"A brightness as of sun or moo

W. A. A. 1, 2; Drama Club 1, 2, 3, 4; "Ni
uary Sixteenth"; Current Events Club 2
Columns 2, 3, 4; College Fellowship 4;
Staff 4; House Council 4.

ADRIENNE BONVOULOIR

"The uttermost of men, who knows the sea in
all its depths."

Secretary-Treasurer of M.A.A. 4; Intramural
Sports 3, 4; Varsity Basketball 3, 4; Current
Events Club 3.

NORMAN BOYER

"Oh, that the Gods should clothe me with such
strength as his."

Intramural Sports 1, 2, 3, 4; J.V. Basketball 3, 4;
Drama Club 3, 4. "Night of January Sixteenth",
"Three-Cornered Moon." Glee Club 4, "Mikado";
Newman Club 3, 4; Yearbook Staff 4; Current
Events Club 3, 4.

MRS. MARTHA BRAWN
"And full of grace is her handicraft."

EDWINA BRENNAN

"Like to the gods in form and comeliness."

Drama Club 4; Commuter's Club 1, 2, 3, 4; New-man Club 4; Yearbook Club 4; Cheerleader 1, 2.

NORMAN BURDICK

"Like to the gods in voice."

President of M. A. A. 4; Intramural Sports 1, 2, 3, 4; Drama Club 4; Glee Club 1, 4; "Christmas Pageant" 2; "Christmas Carol" 3, "Mikado" 4; Taconic Columns 4; College Fellowship 4; Varsity Basketball 3, 4; Yearbook Staff 4; Student Council 4.

NATALIE CARPENTER

"Fair goddess of golden-throned dawn"

W. A. A. 1, 2, 3; Current Events Club 3; Cheer-leader 1, 2; College Fellowship 4; Class Treas-urer 1, 4; College Publicity 3; Class Secretary 3; Yearbook Staff 4; Class VP 2; Dorm Treasurer 2, 3, 4; Dorm Council 2, 3, 4; Drama Club 2, 3, Treasurer 4; "Night of January Sixteenth" 2.

MARTIN COOKISH

"Shaker of the Earth."

Intramural Sports 1, 2, 3, 4; Current Events Club
2, 3, 4.

RUTH CUMMINGS

"A Girl Tall and Divinely Beautiful,"

Drama Club 1, 2; Commuter's Club 1, 2, 3, 4;
Honor Society 2, 3, 4; Class Treasurer 2.

JACQUELINE FERGUSON

"Lo, Thou has shining raiment."

House Council 3; Drama Club 1, 4; Newman Club
2, 3; Secretary 4.

JAMES GAZZANIGA

"And heard the consuls of the gr

Intramural Sports 1, 2; Basketball Mana
Class President 1; Student Council 3; P
Drama Club 1, 2, 4, "Jenny Kissed M
of January Sixteenth"; Current Events C
President 3; Who's Who 4; Newman Clu
Bookstore Manager 3, 4.

DORIS HAMILTON

"A Lovely Child, fair as golden Ap

Commuter's Club 1, 2, 3, 4; Presiden
Secretary 2; Honor Society 2; Secretar
ident 4; Drama Club 2; Glee Club 1
Club 1, 2, 3, 4; College Publicity 3.

SYLVIA HOFSEPIAN

"Fleet as the Breath of the Wir

W. A. A. 1, 2; Commuter's Club 1, 2, 3
dent 4; Honor Society 2, 3, 4; Student
Drama Club 2; Glee Club 1.

MARION HORN

"She is full of intelligence and her heart
is sound."

W. A. A. 1, 2, 3; Sports Leader; Commuter's Club
1, 2; Glee Club 1, 2; Fireside Forum 1, 2; College
Fellowship 4; Vice-President.

NANCY HURLBURT

"There is no more gracious or perfect delight."

W. A. A. 1, 2, 3, 4; Commuter's Club 1,2,3,4; Class
Secretary 4; Honor Society 2, 3; VP 4; Yearbook
Staff 4.

RAYMOND KAVY

"And was Gentle as a Father."

Intramural Sports 3, 4; Upperclass representative 4.

FRED KELLEY

"A name above the gods for cleverness and
intelligence."

Intramural Sports 1, 2, 3, 4; College Publicity 3.

ROBERT KELLY

"A paragon of mankind at planning and
story-telling."

Drama Club 4, "Christmas Carol" 3; Newman
Club 2, 3, 4; Yearbook Staff 4.

FRANK LAMB

"The Achaeans shall noise his fame abroad."

Secretary-Treasurer of M.A.A. 3; Upper-Class
Advisor 4; Art Club 1; "Christmas Carol" 3;
Taconic Columns 3.

GLORIA LEBEL

"Wonder comes o'er me as I look thereon."

W.A.A. 1, 2, 4; VP 3; Drama Club 2, 4; Dorm Council President 4; Student Council 4; Current Events Club 1; Newman Club 1, 2, 3, 4; Cheerleader 1, 2; Who's Who 4.

GEORGE LEONARD

"A man with a mind as wise as the gods."

Intramural Sports 1, 2, 3, 4; Varsity Basketball 1, 2; Varsity Baseball 2; "Christmas Carol" 3; Taconic.Columns 3; Yearbook Staff 4.

ROBERT MARONI

"To give light to the immortals and to mortal men on earth."

Intramural Sports 1, 2, 3, 4; Varsity Basketball 2; JV 1; Varsity Baseball 2; Current Events Club 1; Taconic Columns 1; Editor 2; Elementary School Coach.

PETER MARTINELLI

"A man full of schemes, there never was his match."

Intrumural Sports 1, 2, 3, 4; Varsity Baseball 2; "Christmas Carol" 3.

FUAD NASSIF

"Ye are of the line of men that are sceptered Kings."

Secretary of M. A. A. 2; Intramural Sports 1, 2, 3, 4; Varsity Basketball 1, 2; JV 3, 4; "Christmas Carol" 3; Newman Club 2, 3, 4; VP 3; National Newman Club Conference 3.

ARTHUR O'BRIEN

"Shepherd of the People."

Intramural Sports 1, 2, 3, 4; Class President 3, 4; Upper Class Representative 3; Varsity Basketball Manager 3; Glee Club 1, 2, 4; "Mikado" 4; Current Events Club 2, VP 3; Newman Club 1, 2, 3; President 4; Swampscott Conference 4.

ALLEN PRATT

"For lo it is a good thing to list to a minstrel such as him."

Intramural Sports 2, 3, 4; Taconic Columns 3, 4; College Fellowship 4; College Publicity 3.

CHARLES SANGUINET

"The man without stain and without reproach."

Intramural Sports 1, 2, 3, 4; Current Events Club 2, 3; President 4; Newman Club 1, 2, 3; VP 4; Art Club 1, 2.

ALFRED SOMMER

"A lion hearted man."

Intramural Sports 1, 2, 3, 4; Upper Class Representative, M.A.A. 4; Class VP 3, 4.

MARALYN SPRAGUE

"Whether thou art a goddess or a mortal."

Commuter's Club 1, 2, 3, 4; Honor Society 2, 3, 4; Drama Club 1; Christmas Pageant 2.

PAULINE WAIDLICH

"I see in thee the bright flame of life."

W. A. A. 1, 2; Dorm Council 2; Honor Society 2, 3; Secretary 4; Drama Club 4; Glee Club 1, 2; Taconic Columns 2, Editor 3; Newman Club 1, 2, 3, Treasurer 4; Press Club 3; College Publicity 3.

MARION WALSH

"She is of heart the most blessed beyond all others."

W. A. A. 1, 2, 3, 4; Glee Club 1, 2, 3; Current Events Club 1, 2, 3; Art Club 1, President 2; Taconic Columns 1, 2; Editor 3; College Fellowship 4.

MARY WHITMAN

"Good fortune go with thee."

NANCY WOOLF

"A form dear to the Gods."

W.A.A. 1, 2 3, 4; Glee Club 1, 2, 3, 4; "Mikado" 4; Taconic Columns 1, 2; Editor 3; College Fellowship 4.

This space we humbly dedicate to those who brightened our college lives while they were here and then passed beyond our ken to other fields.

IVY DAY ORATION

Dr. Bowman, Members of the faculty, honored guests:

An astute individual who, no doubt, was philosophically inclined, once made the profound statement that time passes. The wisdom of these words is, unfortunately, too often disregarded, yet the awful truth holds fast. But in its passing, time certainly brings many benefits, for with age certainly should come wisdom, of which we have a concrete example today.

Slightly less than four years ago, our class entered this institution of higher learning. At the time the great majority of us were quite immature individuals and, I must confess, quite devoid of the lore which a supposedly well-educated individual should possess to better himself in the world of today.

Traditionally, class day marks the emergence of the aforementioned naive individuals from the supposedly cloistered, semi-protected existence they have been leading into the realm of reality, or if you will, into the hard, cruel world. From this moment on we must endeavor to reconcile principle with expediency, supposition with fact, the hypothetical with the actual in our chosen profession as teachers.

But what do we find in the world into which we have emerged? Does not this very epithet—teacher—connote an unfavorable meaning in itself? Webster defines the word teacher as one "who guides the study of others;" and according to the same authority an educator is one who "develops and cultivates mentally and morally". Which is of greater service to his country, the one who merely "guides" or the one who "develops and cultivates"? And for whom should this function be exercised—merely for the pupils during the day in school, or for the community as a whole?

The adherents of the policy that a teacher's sole duty lies to his pupils and that this duty consists only of guiding the studies of his charges have made the teacher, in far too many cases, an insignificant, innocuous, and insipid individual who is afraid to speak his mind on controversial issues for fear of the consequences which might ensue. The teacher should be a leader in his community, a shaper of public opinion, and a guardian of that most precious of all traits—an objective, logical viewpoint. The teacher should take it upon himself to be not only the "guider" of young children, but a "developer and cultivator"—an educator in every sense of the word, not only of his charges, but of his compeers as well.

Today the teacher is faced with a seemingly insoluble dilemma: either to remain in his "sanctum sanctorum", safe from the inevitable criticism and difficulties brought about by outspokeness; or to emerge from this rustication, this seclusion, and endeavor to fulfill his duty to his community, to his country and to his own conscience.

But wherein lies this duty, you well may ask?

At present, the mass of the populace of the United States are in a state of nervous tension which they seek to aleviate by some painless, effortless method. Everywhere, panacea are being offered by various persons who are capitalizing on this sense of insecurity. Books which deal with the problems of living a peaceful life and of gaining security are best-sellers. Obscure cults which purport to delve into the supernatural are everywhere springing into prominence. What is more important, this state of tension is causing us to regress in both our moral and ethical beliefs, and is, moreover, bringing about a change in the hierarchy of the values which many people hold.

No longer is the teacher, or any other educated person, looked up to and respected as an individual

—Continued on Page 47

THE IVY POEM

The leaving grates against my mind,
the awful ending of the all
that we have known-finality.
I cannot see the glowing world
with arms that seek to take and hold my heart
I only know that I shall lose a friend.
Perhaps the sentiment is bare,
perhaps I haven't got the stuff
to face the stern realities of life;
perhaps, but no, it isn't that;--
it's just the memories, the dreams
the quiet moments lost in pensive thought
that suddenly engulf my mind,
recalling all that was and is
and cannot be again.
They say tomorrow never comes
and yet tomorrow with its awe full end,
its grim excitement closing a door
is coming, --now
Goodbye to what has been
my heart will never know that happiness again.

What is a college?
Old and tired walls surrounding ancient classrooms,
musty with the smell of learning;
Scuff-marked halls,
still echoing with voices that were stilled a quarter
                        century ago;
Terraces with grass that blooms anew each spring,
vying with the dusty textbooks gathered there;
Adolescent nick-names scrawled on window casements;
Granite steps worn smooth and shiny
by shoes forever changing in their style;
Youth in baggy sweaters and five o'clock shadow
taking notes or doodling
or dreaming--- of the end of class;
Instructors lecturing from notes and wondering where
                        the scholars went;
Youth wondering, worrying, cramming for exams;
Youth loving, losing, taking margin notes;
snapshots, hopes, ambitions, ---immaturity;
The long and thankless job of moulding character;
A way of life inshrined in all the hearts
that ever beat within those ivy covered walls.

History of The

If a newcomer to the diminutive municipality of North Adams were to stroll up Church Street, he would pass by a small cluster of stately buildings which a weather-beaten sign proclaims to all to be the State Teachers College. There, on a certain fateful day in September, 1949, a group of ninety-six eager young men and women entered upon a severe program of studies designed to create from the crude, malleable ore of naive, immature adolescents the polished, erudite pedagogues that grace contemporary institutions of edification. Their personal trials, tribulations, glories, and triumphs, although worthy, are too miscellaneous and vast a collection to present herewith, but their combined intellectual and social progress may, perhaps, be suggested by the following class history.

This was a time of great stress in the world. The economic structures of nations the world over were tottering, the threat of communism was looming more and more ominous, and a genuine crisis was developing in Palestine over the conflicts between the Arabs and Israeli.

But history is always history, and our minds were busy absorbing knowledge in more immediate fields. A casual onlooker might raise an eyebrow at the sight of freshmen scurrying about the campus busily examining the bark of trees, but we were oblivious to any ridicule, for those tree maps just had to be completed. We had our first glimpse of the erudite Dr. Freel, whom we were to know better and better as we progressed through N. A. S. T. C., the intrepid Miss Underhill, and that of the inimitable Wily Willie Malone.

Not all of our time, however, was spent in pursuit of that fleeting imp, knowledge. We still found time for extra-curricular activities. The men began their four-year domination of intramural sports, as "Freel's Frosh" swept all before them in the football league. We mingled with one another at the Freshman Reception, and somehow managed to survive a tumultuous election in which Jim Gazzaniga edged out the incomparable (remember him?) Jim Young, Esq. A few stalwart members of our class were members of the New England Championship basketball team and still others starred in "Jenny Kissed Me'.'

Our sophomore year brought back a group slightly diminished, a trifle more sophisticated, but with that thirst for knowledge still unslaked. Somehow we staggered through Physical Science, Economic Geography, English, and American Literature, and drank deeply from other fountains of knowledge. Who of us that were present shall ever forget the day Charlie Chaplin appeared to do an experiment for us? We all strove

Class of 1953

to emulate Demosthenes in an incomparable Public Speaking Course, but nevertheless still found the time to answer the call of the social world. Our various talents were spent in promoting the Sophomore Prom and various other social affairs. Still others of us starred in "The Night of January Sixteenth".

When, once again, we returned, this time as Jaunty Juniors, we found a group greatly reduced, but more nearly approaching that pinnacle of complaisance, and the aforementioned thirst for knowledge still unsatiated. This year found us at last embarking upon the perception of the methodology which forms the background that any self-respecting dominie must have to be accomplished in his profession, it seems. Those of us who elected Guidance as our major were introduced to the rudiments of that fascinating field. Soon we were immersed completely in the "busy work" for which the junior year is justly famous. Yet, underneath all our grumbling, beneath this blind groping, there beat within our breasts burning desires to become modern reincarnations of Virrotino de Feltre, Maria Montessori, and who knows, even Henry Pestalozzi.

This was the year the Grover's Gaza Globetrotters made their long trek from Mecca for a successful appearance against the JV's. And this year also saw us sponsoring the Junior-Senior Prom, winning the Stunt Nite competition for the second time, and romping through the "Christmas Carol."

Our senior year saw a compact group return to brave the proving grounds of Mark Hopkins Training School. We were a mere shadow of the unruly mob that had first entered here four years previously, yet those of us who were left were beginning to approach the standard of leadership expected of us. The Guidance Majors had their three afternoons in the Clinic, where they, too, began to put their principles into practice. We also thought our way through a Philosophy of Education, and amazed veteran pedagogues wherever we took our field week. We also struggled through Tests and Measurements, Mental Hygiene, and Philosophy.

The Future Teachers of America, an organization dedicated to the resuscitation of tired minds, was founded in this year. Those of us who were musically inclined blossomed out in the *Mikado*.

Gradually, even imperceptibly we changed; we settled down, and in adapting ourselves to greater responsibilities, lost a great deal of the previously mentioned immaturity. Perhaps, in the process, even becoming teachers.

UNDERCLASSMEN

The Junior Class

We came back to the College on the Hill in September, exuberant over the thought that we were no longer "silly sophomores" but now upper classmen. We faced the year ahead with vitality and hope, but as the weeks passed we found ourselves over-loaded with Plato, Methods, and the Training School. We managed once more to survive exams with the help of a little cramming and a pack or two of cigarettes. In spite of our schedule and lack of adequate free time we were able to keep our class spirit high and to participate vigorously in extra curricular activities. We supplied the Mikado with the best of our talent, as well as providing the basketball team with skillful players and a loyal and loud cheering section. We sponsored a Winter Carnival Weekend with high hopes that the occasion will become traditional at N. A. S. T. C. We helped to plan and present the annual Junior-Senior Prom as a finale to our third year at the college. For us it has been a full and eventful year, and we look forward to our vacation as a time to digest our Methods, mull over Plato, and find respite from the training school. We hope to return in the fall with our never-ceasing vitality and with the realization that at last we have reached our goal—to be STATELY SENIORS.

The Sophomore Class

"United we stand; divided we fall!" This was the motto of the sophomore class when we returned to N. A. S. T. C. in September. Although the smallest class in the school, we were determined to make our mark. With high spirits we entered into the many school activities and delved into our studies. Overwhelmed by the amount of knowledge we had yet to learn, we nevertheless struggled through. We became scientists, weather forecasters, artsts, poets, and musicians, all rolled into one. By the end of the year, we considered ourselves extremely wise and capable of doing almost anything.

But don't think that all we did was study! We had our social life, too. Our smiling personalities were to be seen at the various club meetings, the socials, the basketball games, and in the cast of the *Mikado*. We enthusiastically did our part in supporting all of the school functions. Our crowning achievement in this line was the Sophomore Prom. Through the teamwork of the class and our advisor, Dr. Semon, and the leadership of the class officers, we showed the school that quantity isn't necessary to success. Having managed to complete the school year, we expectantly look to the future and to being jolly, jolly juniors.

The Freshman Class

Although our little group entered N. A. S. T. C. in a state of confusion, it was not long before we became an organized class. Names became familiar to our ears and certain sights to our eyes. The strangeness faded and the warmth of our new friendships led us to feel that we were established. With a newly installed set of officers we faced our first big problem, The Freshman Halloween Dance. It proved to be less of a problem than we had imagined however and we can feel justified in calling it a success. Small as our group was, we contributed one little maid to the Mikado and three big men to the varsity basketball team. Then the battle of exams came into view. Emerging from the battle as victors, we appeared in the classrooms for the second semester. We supplied the Winter Carnival with its queen and two members of her court and were represented among the attendants to the May Queen, too. We were little but mighty at Stunt Nite and more than held our own on Class Day. So, with the initial stage of our journey behind us, we look with eager eyes to the path that lies ahead.

ACTIVITIES

Honor Society

The Frank Fuller Murdock Honor Society is composed of students whose qualities of scholorship and leadership are above the average. The society concerns itself with attempting to instill those qualities in the rest of the student body. A combined lecture and social program was held in the spring. Doris Hamilton serves as president.

Student Council

The Student Council is the governing body in N. A. S. T. C. To the council falls the task of originating and administering school policies. The council consists of school officers, class presidents and organization heads. Council officers for 1952-53 were James Gazzaniga, Fritz Brown, and Paula Coons.

Dorm Council

The Dorm Council determines and applies the rules and regulations that govern the women's dormitory. Like the Student Council, the Dorm Council is composed of dorm officers and class presidents. This years council, led by Gloria LeBell has made many forward steps in the process of improving and modernizing the existing regulations.

M. A. A.

Norman Burdick, President
With firm resolve and dread
intent
Asserted one September day
That he'd reform the M.A.A.
He struggled all through the
year
To mend it's ways and yet I
fear
That next years class shall
more or less
Discover it's the same old
mess.

W. A. A.

The W.A.A. functions as a social
and athletic group. Athletically it
sponsors hikes, field hockey, swim-
ming, basketball, and badminton. So-
cially the group gives a square dance
and games carnival annually. Officers
for 1952-53 are Harriet Beck, Dot
Nordberg and Charlotte Smith. Miss
Beth Weston is faculty advisor.

Commuters Club

The commuters, with Sylvia Hofsepian as President, began the year
by undertaking a vast civic improve-
ments program. New curtains were
added to lend that "homey touch", and
slip covers were also helpful in
brightening up the commuters' room.
The girls, aside from their domestic
duties, found time to sponsor their
yearly social affair, and to provide
refreshments for several other gath-
erings.

Taconic Columns

Taconic Columns is a bimonthly newspaper published by the students so they may express themselves in a literary way. The issues include news items and writeups of various social activities held at the college or of interest to the students. Regular columnists cover standard items. The paper is sent to former students serving in the armed forces.

The Newman Club

The Newman Club, headed this year by Arthur O'Brien, dedicated itself to the task of increasing and clarifying inter-religious understanding. Services and discussions were held that greatly aided members in solving the problems of modern living. The club also held several dances and parties throughout the year.

College Fellowship

Our newest Extra Cirrucular star rose above the horizon this fall. Several guest speakers were invited to speak to the group on topics of vital importance to young men and women. The club will prove an invaluable aid in adjusting to the present day world.

The Footlighters

The doughty dramatists, aided by Dr Dennett as advisor and led by Jack Pozzias president, again engaged in their annual struggle to bring culture to S. T. C. After enrolling "en masse" to aid in the "Mikado", the thespians showed their mettle in "An Old Lady Shows Her Medals", and their yearly full scale production. Three cheers for a job well done.

The Music Club

The presentation of the "Mikado" in November of 1953 by the college and the enthusiasm with which it was received led to the founding of the Music Club. The organization presents musical programs to the college and has sponsored periods of listening to selected recorded music. The highlight of the clubs activities was a combined concert and social program. Mark Ryan leads the group and Miss Boyden is advisor.

The Current Events Club

The Current Events Club, by discussion and debate, aims to stimulate interest in current affairs in both student body and faculty. This year the club has been fortunate in having as guest speakers, Atty. Lilly and Rev. Dr. Cole in a pre-election debate, and City Manager Harp in a talk about city government. Numerous discussions have been held at regular meetings and pertinent film strips have been shown.

The Odyssey Staff

Into our lives, one November day, came a

new responsibility. We had been chosen

to develop, write, and publish our

yearbook. Now at the end of our

struggle, we wish to thank all

who aided us; we could not

have finished the job with-

out your assistance

Graham Andrews
Arthur O'Brien
Robert Kelly
Janet Bishop
Natalie Carpenter
Pauline Waidlich
Edwina Brennan
Nancy Hurlbit
Charles Sanguinet

Miss Mary Underhill
Faculty Advisor

SPORTS

THE VARSITY

Basketball

The 1952-53 basketball season at N.A.S.T.C can be generally summed up in one short sentence. "Nobody defeated us at home and we defeated nobody away from home". Th statement, like most generalizations however, is not quite true and tends to be misleading. We did defeat Westfield at Westfield in a non-conference game, but the important fact is that we played only five games away from home all season. This might lead the uninformed reader to suspect that w are homebodies or develop homesickness while traveling. Neither supposition has any basis in fact however, the schedule just worked out that way. This was a good year though, no matter how we look at it. We finished a strong second in the New England Teachers College Conference and ended the season with a ten and four won-lost record. The squad was bolstered this year by| three very capable freshmen: Pat Grady

JUNIOR VARSITY

OUR FAN CLUB

Charlie Perinick, and Ed Pierson. This new blood combined with the talented behavior of George Jarck, Fred Hubbard, George Petropolus, Bill McLaren, and Steve Cozzaglio, proved to be too much for the opposition.

Great hopes are held for next season when, barring unforseen developments, the college will field the same veteran squad. May they realize their potentials and bring North Adams another championship. Any discussion of basketball at S.T.C. would not be complete without mention of our junior varsity. Playing unwatched preliminaries week after week one would think they would lose some of their zest for the game. Nothing is farther from the truth. Scores in record books will tell you that they were beaten in almost as many games as they won, but actually no team is ever beaten until it gives up trying. The Junior Varsity never gave up! They deserve our wholehearted thanks for a job well done. While thank-yous are being handed out we should express our appreciation for our able Cheerleaders and loyal fans. Your support was invaluable.

THE CHEERLEADERS

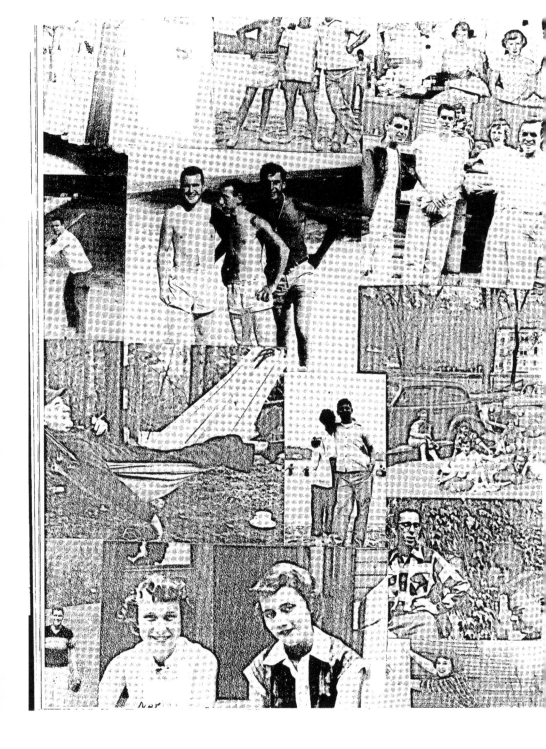

1953

SENIORS

Andrews, Graham	40 Elm Street, Adams, Mass.
Bennett, Carolyn	45 Taunton Avenue, Mattapan, Mass.
Bishop, Janet	34 Hayes Street, Lynn, Mass.
Bonvoulair, Adrien	78 Yale Street, North Adams, Mass.
Boyer, Norman	586 Union Street, North Adams, Mass.
Brawn, Martha (Mrs.)	2 Avenue B, Turners Falls, Mass.
Brennan, Edwina	504 Church Street, North Adams, Mass.
Burdick, Norman	Main Street, Charlemont, Mass.
Carpenter, Natalie	127 High Street, Greenfield, Mass.
Cookish, Martin	14 Bond Street, North Adams, Mass.
Cummings, Ruth	166 Bracewell Ave., North Adams, Mass.
Erkelens, Cornelia	95 Glendale Road, Sharon, Mass.
Ferguson, Jacquelyn	138 Newell Street, Pittsfield, Mass.
Gallant, Margaret (Mrs.)	Nourses Road, Lanesboro, Mass.
Gazzaniga, James	219 Church Street, North Adams, Mass.
Hamilton, Doris	East Road, Clarksburg, Mass.
Hofsepian, Sylvia	188 Pleasant Street, North Adams, Mass.
Horn, Marion	520 Church Street, North Adams, Mass.
Hurlbut, Nancy	6 Rich Street, North Adams, Mass.
Jenkins, Carol	Apple Valley Rd., Ashfield, Mass.
Jones, Albert	88 Rutland Street, Watertown, Mass.
Kavey, Raymond	417 North Street, Pittsfield, Mass.
Kelley, Fred	260 Springside Avenue, Pittsfield, Mass.
Kelly, Robert	19 Pine Street, Pittsfield, Mass.
Klein, Lois (Mrs.)	East Chatham, New York.
Lamb, Frank	Depot Street, Cheshire, Mass.
LeBel, Gloria	28 Summit Avenue, Salem, Mass.
Leonard, George	246 First Street, Pittsfield, Mass.
Maroni, Robert	372 Ashland Street, North Adams, Mass.
Martinelli, Peter	34 Dartmouth Street, Pittsfield, Mass.
Nassif, Fuad	831/2 Howland Avenue, Adams, Mass.
O'Brien, Arthur	82 Park Avenue, North Adams, Mass.
Pratt, Allen	41 Woodleigh Avenue, Greenfield, Mass.
Principe, Gennaro	227 Fern Street, Pittsfield, Mass.
Reardon, Dorothy (Mrs.)	194 Wendall Avenue, Pittsfield, Mass.
Sanguinet, Charles	17 Laural Avenue, North Adams, Mass.
Sommer, Alfred	71 Howland Avenue, Adams, Mass.
Sprague, Marilyn	3 Hoosac Court, North Adams, Mass.
Waidlich, Pauline	Millers Falls, Mass.
Walsh, Marion	1641 North Street, Pittsfield, Mass.
Whitman, Mary (Mrs.)	74 Windsor Avenue, Pittsfield, Mass.
Woolf, Nancy	441 Liberty Street, Rockland, Mass.

JUNIORS

Aitchison, Elizabeth	316 South Mountain Rd., Pittsfield, Mass.
Anderson, Donald	18 Hall Street, Williamstown, Mass.
Arnold, Dorothy	422 Rochester Street, Fall River, Mass.
Atkinson, Peggy Lou	Tempast Knob Terr., Wareham, Mass.
Austin, Patricia	521 Pleasant Street, So. Weymouth, Mass.
Babcock, Elizabeth Ann	66 Beach Street, Greenfield, Mass.
Brown, Fritz	779 Salem Street, So. Groveland, Mass.
Call, Douglas	Colrain, Mass.
Cozzaglio, Stephen	23 Lyman Street, North Adams, Mass.

Coons, Paula	10 Harrison Avenue, Williamstown, Mass.
Daly, Barbara	91 Boardman Avenue, Melrose, Mass.
Demo, Lucille	8 Spring Street, North Adams, Mass.
Fitzgerald, Patricia	17 Thatcher Road, Glouscester, Mass.
Gallipeau, Irene	251 Springside Street, Pittsfield, Mass
Graves, Rita	Union Street, Montague, Mass.
Hamilton, Blair	81 Hathaway Street, North Adams, Mass.
Hester, Mary	303 Grove Street, Westwood, Mass.
Hubbard, Fred	Ferry Street, Marshfield, Mass.
Lowe, Scott	39 Montana Street, North Adams, Mass.
McCarron, Eugene	34 Page Street, Rivere, Mass.
Miller, Anne	353 Eagle Street, North Adams, Mass.
Molloy, Julia	16 Quincy Street, North Adams, Mass.
Nordberg Dorothy	140 Branch Street, Mansfield, Mass.
Oakes, Gary	Burdickville, Mass.
O'Conner, James	51 State Street, New Bedford, Mass.
Payne, Nancy	845 Main Street, Holden, Mass.
Peck, Harriet	County Street, West Wareham, Mass.
Petropulous, George	96 Corinth Street, North Adams, Mass.
Pillsbury, Jo Anne	73 Dodge Avenue, Pittsfield, Mass.
Pozzi, John	36 Porter Street, North Adams, Mass.
Rizzo, Alfonso	103 Harbor Street, Lynn, Mass.
Robinson, Laura	15 Pearl Street, Adams, Mass.
Rubin, Elliot	33 Porter Street, North Adams, Mass.
Ryan, Mark	26 Westminster Street, Pittsfield, Mass.
Souza, Ellen	154 Pitman Street, New Bedford, Mass.
Tovani, Joan C.	14 Nelson Street, North Adams, Mass.
Utley, Hazel	62 Gray Street, Amheart, Mass.
Wenzel, June P.	311 Main Street, Fair Haven, Mass.
White, Leona	13 Main Street, E. Northfield, Mass.
Whitman, Rachel	1105 North Street, Pittsfield, Mass.
Wilk, Josephine	Cottage Street, Housatonic, Mass.
Wood, Beverly Ann	82 Grove Street, Leeds, Mass.

SOPHOMORES

Andrews, Kay Janet	40 Elm Street, Adams, Mass.
Bosma, Irma	30 Newell Street, Pittsfield, Mass.
Boyer, Rosaline	18 Richview Terrace, North Adams, Mass.
Dunton, Marilyn	77 Yale Street, North Adams, Mass.
Helfrich, Bernard	77 Butler Street, Lawrence, Mass.
Hofsepian, Marion	188 Pleasant Street, North Adams, Mass.
Hurley, Carol	27 Veasie Street, North Adams, Mass.
Jarck, George	270 East Main Street, North Adams, Mass.
Lockwood, Ann	16 Barth Street, North Adams, Mass.
Love, David	New Ashford, Mass.
McLaren, William	215 N. Summer Street, Adams, Mass.
McNeil, Margaret	277 Medford Street, Somerville, Mass.
Meagher, Judith	82 Hawthorne Street, Pittsfield, Mass.
Merrigan, Michael	453 West Main Street, North Adams, Mass.
Murphy, Janet	12 Estes Street, North Adams, Mass.
Owczaiski, Frances	14 Richmond Lane, Adams, Mass.

Pastermark, Virginia	6 Linden Street, Adams, Mass.
Righi, Angelo	671 Curran Highway, North Adams, Mass.
Rotti, Robert	12 Argyle Road, Arlingon, Mass.
Rugg, Constance	Southfield, Mass.
Sherman, Mary	20 Moorland Street, Williamstown, Mass.
Smith, Charlotte	53 Lincoln Street, Hudson, Mass.
Tanguay, Regina	214 North Summer Street, Adams, Mass.
Daignault, Beverly	Charlemont, Mass.

FRESHMEN

Bachette, John Jr.	Silver Street, Sheffield, Mass.
	% Petersens
Belding, Elizabeth	34 Elm Street, North Adams, Mass.
Bowes, Carol Lou	32 West End Terrace, North Adams, Mass.
Comonetti, Carol	100 North Street, North Adams, Mass.
Damon, Joan	Haydenville, Mass.
DeMadonna, Joanne	188 East Main Street, North Adams, Mass.
Gilmore, Sally	43 Fredrick Street, North Adams, Mass.
Grady, Patrick	99 Francis Avenue, Pittsfield, Mass.
Holloway, Esther	343 State Street, North Adams, Mass.
Jones, George	279 Houghton Street, North Adams, Mass.
Keyes, Ruth	Leyden Road, Greenfield, Mass.
Kunstler, Joan	17 Leninton Street, Roslindale, Mass.
LaPlante, Frances	South Vernon, Mass.
LaTaif, Joyce	99 Gallup Street, North Adams, Mass.
Lopez, Maria	Maple Street, Northfield, Mass.
Mello, Edward	Vineyard Haven, Mass.
Murley, Patricia	13 Cypress Street, Greenfield, Mass.
Neil, Elizabeth	Main Street, Sagamore, Mass.
Pecheqlys, Mary	27 Church Street, Pittsfield, Mass.
Perenick, Charles	54 Chase Avenue, North Adams, Mass.
Pierson, Edward Jr.	39 Maple Street, Williamstown, Mass.
Quadrozzi, Thomas	42 Longview Terrace, Pittsfield, Mass.
Saulnier, Wilfred	71 Liberty Street, North Adams, Mass.
Stewart, Dorothea	10 Merkle Street, Holyoke, Mass.
Tobin, Thomas	99 Grove Street, Adams, Mass.
Walker, Joan	White Creek, New York.

Ivy Day Oration

Continued from Page 22—

who has partaken deeply of the fount of knowledge. On the contrary, he is today looked upon with suspicion and distrust as a fomentor and disseminator of theories which threaten to overthrow the government.

And what has occasioned this distrust, you ask? The reason is readily discernable. Largely, it is the result of the insidious propaganda being diffused by a group of self-seeking, glory-hunting hypocrites who have donned the mantle of crusaders fighting the fire-breathing dragon of communism. The state of mass hysteria which grips the country is greatly the result of the actions of these rumor-mongers in their self-righteous campaigns to root out the evils of what is loosely termed Marxism, whatever the guise in which it may appear.

Far too many people have fallen victim to the Machiavellian machinations of these modern inquisitors. All that is needed to defame the character of any man is to couple to his name the vituperative stigma of communism, and at once he is classified as a pariah.

However, this is not to imply that there are no virtuous, patriotic men of high principle engaged in this struggle to seek out communism in our government. But has not this campaign grown out of proportion to its actual danger when it threatens to destroy the very liberties which our forefathers died for? And would it not be infinitely more logical to face communism, to dissect it, to attempt to understand it so as to combat it more effectively, than to treat it as some odious, shadowy specter, the very mention of which is sufficient to bring about gasps of horror and implications of contamination?

But then you ask, what is that which we have to fear? In the words of the immortal Franklin Delano Roosevelt, ". . . the only thing we have to fear is fear itself—nameless, unreasoning, unjustified terror which paralyzes needed efforts to convert retreat into advance." We should attempt to face our problems vigorously and confidently instead of seeking some magical cure-all which will avail us nothing. Through the years, our democratic system of government has weathered successfully the stress and strain of vast expansion of territory and of bitter sectional conflict; has endured the vicissitudes of international wars and entangling foreign relations. Ah, but how have these problems been met? By the throttling and persecution of minorities; by the assertion of the premise that a man is guilty until he is proved innocent? The evidence is very much to the contrary. America has endured, has prospered because of the tolerance of minorities and through the attempt to understand the viewpoint of others; the result of which has been the after attainment of a unified nation after the differences of opinion have been ironed out.

Today, the teacher is in a position to do his country a great service by speaking out courageously against these forces which threaten our freedoms, by becoming an educator in every sense of the word. The teacher has the opportunity to become a leader in this fight for the very essence of our democracy.

Ah, but how many esteemed pedagogues will or would become leaders in this fight against injustices? How many instead would sacrifice their personal principles for the doubtful security they gain by muteness and conformity?

Unless the teacher accepts this challenge, and attempts to fulfill his duty to both his country, and what is more important, to himself: the title applied to him will be a meaningless and oprobrious misnomer.